SAINT PETERS

St Petersburg will soon be marking its three-hundredth anniversary. When admiring its splendour, you are constantly struck by the thought that this museum-city teeming with historical associations is in essence still very young. Here history comes across not as the remote past, but as something close, intimately bound up with the present day and with your own life. You picture quite vividly the huge, impetuous, indomitable figure of Peter taking his first decisive strides along the marshy bank of the Neva, Ulyanov-Lenin stealing furtively through the dark streets in the autumn of 1917 to reach Smolny, or the exhausted inhabitants of besieged Leningrad slipping and sliding down the icy embankments to draw water from the Neva...

This is the main difference between St Petersburg and other major cultural centres around the world and one of the secrets of its attraction. The history of St Petersburg does not go back into the mists of time like that of Rome, say, or even Moscow. It can be grasped in the mind in its entirety, although it is replete with epoch-making events. The contemplation of the past, which inevitably results from viewing the beauty of the city elevates one above the everyday bustle and generates a host of profound impressions and thoughts.

St Petersburg is in its way a unique city, having appeared almost instantly to a single, deliberate plan, becoming the highest embodiment of human will, the triumph of creative inspiration and intensive labour. By the end of its first century of existence, St Petersburg was one of the finest cities in Europe. St Petersburg is a dream come true, an object lesson in history closely linked with the present.

For the Russians, St Petersburg is a European city. When he conceived its construction, Peter the Great thought of it becoming first and foremost the maritime gateway of Russia, "a window to Europe". The Tsar invited a host of foreign architects to work on the new capital, and it is above all to them and those who followed in their footsteps – Trezzini, Rastrelli, Quarenghi, Cameron, Montferrand and the rest – that the city owes its appearance. Architecturally the city took up the finest achievements of European urban construction. Yet, as has often been remarked, the magnificent edifices erected here by noted Italian, French or British architects acquired some special expansive quality uniquely typical of Russia.

Apart from architecture, various sciences and trades, arts and fashionable European goods came into Russia through St Petersburg. While the city was the capital, it was home to very large numbers of foreigners and European attitudes were indeed dominant. On the other hand, visitors from abroad in Catherine's time, for example, observed that, along with features reminiscent of elite society in Paris or London, one could also see in St Petersburg merchants in Asiatic dress and long-bearded peasants in sheepskin coats and fur-hats. And even the borrowings from abroad took on a new, purely Russian aspect here.

No, St Petersburg was always what it remains today: a city that combines within it Russia and Europe. For foreigners coming here now as tourists it is certainly not the West, especially after several decades of enforced isolation from foreign influences. For them it is, however, the key to understanding the mysterious Russian mind and the "Eastern Empire" that covers one seventh of the Earth's land surface. St Petersburg with its aristocratically noble appearance, its "European-like" restrained character is more approachable and understandable that the blatantly multifarious Moscow with its tempestuous rhythms and headlong pursuit of modernity, or the rest of Russia, which might in many ways be said to be still slumbering.

Peter the Great, having resolved to bring his country closer to Europe, sought an exit to the sea. From that point of view, the site he chose, where the Neva flows into the Gulf of Finland, was ideal. For the construction of a city (still more a capital), however, the natural conditions were, to say the least, not favourable: a harsh climate and terrain that was marshy and therefore flat and uninspiring. The apparent disadvantages of the setting were, however, brilliantly exploited by architects. The abundance of water provided the finest possible adornment for St Petersburg – without it a city built of brick and stone would be too austere, even somewhat gloomy. The rather featureless landscape made it possible to construct impeccably straight streets, while the relatively tall buildings stood out to advantage on the level expanse. This fact was noted back in the eighteenth century by the poet and scientist Mikhail Lomonosov: "Nature has provided an even, low-lying land surface, as if deliberately for the placement of man-made mountains as a demonstration of the immense might of Russia, because although there are no natural eminences here, huge buildings soar up in their stead."

By present-day standards, of course, the buildings in the central part of St Petersburg are not particularly tall, but that is more of a virtue: they are just high enough to create an impression of compact beauty without overwhelming the spectator. The one- and two-storey Moscow of the nobility was swept away in Soviet times in the rush to create an "exemplary capital", while the buildings of St Petersburg, whose three to seven storeys once seemed excessively tall, now fully accord with conceptions of a harmonious, human-scale urban environment – even the cars and buses of the modern world fit in well with them.

St Petersburg is notable for everything being thought out and in proportion. It is above all a "regular" city. Yet, for all the rational planning, there is no feeling of monotony at all. The dense rows of houses forming the streets themselves delight the eye with their variety of design and colour. But the city achieves aesthetic perfection and a particular impressiveness through the presence of dominant architectural features that rise above the general mass of buildings. The golden spires and domes of the Admiralty, SS Peter and Paul Cathedral, the Naval Cathedral of St Nicholas and, finally, St Isaac's (which is visible from outside the city) not only enliven the general cityscape, moderating its northern austerity, but also intensify the sense of integrity and harmony.

Striking unity coupled with powerful, memorable individual elements is one of the most attractive features of the city on the Neva.

One further very important peculiarity of St Petersburg is the way in which the man-made architecture with its precise, rational lines successfully combines with expanses of water that embody the dynamic unpredictability of the elements. It should be said that Le Blond's original conception for the centre of the city, on Vasilyevsky Island, envisaged the creation of rectangular blocks divided by "lines" numbered like the avenues in New York. Even then, the plan called for canals rather that streets between the blocks, which would, of course, have introduced a picturesque element and reduced the impression of monotony.

In the event, the centre of the city shifted to the left bank of the Neva. The final layout of the city is strikingly simple and appealing. The "trident" of three main roads radiating out from the Admiralty also has something geometrical about it, but at the same time it is too elaborate as to be immediately noticeable. Besides which, the numerous rivers and canals that literally dissect the whole of St Petersburg give it a vitality that a city built in accordance with a single concept would clearly lack.

The watery element plays a special role in the appearance of St Petersburg. It is impossible to imagine a description of the city that does not mention the Neva. It is not only the central waterway, but also a living nerve setting the rhythm of life for the whole city. Of course, the Neva is a northern river and its waters do not prompt the same associations with refreshing coolness, bathing and the irrigation of crops that arise in the south with, say, the Amu-Darya or the Nile. It has a certain severity, restraint and even epic solemnity about it. But the granite-clad Neva, bearing its waters to the sea year after year, has its own unique poetry. The river itself would, of course, be simply dull without its granite finery, without the magnificent buildings lining its banks, the finely proportioned columns of the Exchange, the indescribably stirring curves of its bridges and, finally, the spire of the SS Peter and Paul Cathedral glistening in the sun.

The Neva is also a fairly broad river. You immediately realize the positive effect of this, if you compare it to the Seine, for example. Without disparaging the attraction of the Parisian river, it becomes obvious at once that it loses out to the Neva because of its narrowness which renders it somehow more prosaic. In Paris the opposite bank is clearly seen and looks less

The Spit of Vasilyevsky Island

The Cathedral of SS Peter and Paul ▶

romantic, mysterious and fascinating than in St Petersburg. At the same time, the Neva is not so wide that the other bank is simply lost to view; it seems to be just sufficiently remote to allow one's thoughts to escape from the mundane and plunge into the contemplation of eternal beauty.

Water gives St Petersburg a sense of space and spaciousness. The Neva is highly suited to the panoramic viewing of Classical architecture, while the smaller rivers and canals create an impression of intimacy and mystery. Panoramic pictures are the most effective and most typical views of St Petersburg. Take a look, for example, at the panorama of the city that opens up from the Trinity Bridge. There is a striking harmony of all proportions: the line of austere buildings in different colours frozen along the flatness of the constantly moving water that is emphasized by the embankments; the smooth arcade of the Palace Bridge with its variegated flow of traffic; the white patches of pleasure cruisers on the mysteriously dark surface of the water; the airy shapes making up the tower of the pale blue Kunstkammer building; the solid, Classical colonnade of the Exchange giving an integrity to the ensemble on the Spit of Vasilyevsky Island. Finally, from this point, there is a particularly fine view of the spire of the SS Peter and Paul Cathedral with its angel soaring above the squat strip of dark red fortress wall and somehow echoing the sailing-ship on the spire of the Admiralty, another symbol of the city. An impression of ideal balance and beauty can be obtained by anyone here – it does not even require a particularly poetic mood.

Or, to give another example, the view towards the Neva from the little bridge across the Winter Canal at Millionnaya Street, looking through Velten's hanging gallery linking the Old Hermitage to the Hermitage Theatre. The perfectly straight line of the narrow canal, its dark, shifting water hemmed in by granite on both sides, carries the eye, obedient to the laws of perspective, into the distance, to the span of the arch above the charming curved line of the bridge and to the rectangular passage to the left. And there bursting out in the sunshine, in contrast to the precise geometry of the canal, is an exceptionally beautiful view of the seemingly infinite Neva with the bright patches of buildings on the opposite bank steeped in some very special blend of air and light far removed from ordinary reality.

The bridges of St Petersburg are a poetic theme in their own right. There are many of them in the city and they delight the eye with their unusual designs, sculptural decoration, distinctive lamps, elegant cast-iron railings or simply their flowing shapes forming an eloquent contrast with the straight lines of the embankments. Indeed it is impossible to imagine the glorious ensemble of St Petersburg without bridges – the broad drawbridges across the Neva, the Anichkov Bridge on Nevsky Prospekt with Klodt's memorable horses, and the little, humpback bridges that unexpectedly appear around a bend, decorated with lions or griffins that bring joy to passers-by. Yet even if the bridges themselves are not particularly striking, they are almost always quietly present in our favourite views of the city.

St Petersburg is a remarkable place at any time of year and in almost any weather. A certain charm can be found even in November when the black, gnarled trunks of the leafless trees stand out against the yel-

6

low walls of Classical buildings, when the sky is almost continuously overcast and the asphalt still wet from the last drizzly shower of rain, when you can see from end to end of the Summer Gardens, deserted without the Minervas and Pomonas that have been crated up for the winter and looking small and sad. There is an air of elegiac melancholy about such sights.

Winter in St Petersburg, as in any northern, maritime city, is depressing not so much because of the frosts, as because of the sharp, penetrating winds and, especially, the darkness. The days are short and people go to work and return home by the light of street lamps. In winter the city draws few tourists.

But in the midst of it there are days in January when the weather comes just right and the wintry city simply glows. The dome of St Isaac's burns in the icy sky, the fluffy, snow-covered branches of trees take on a silvery hue and the white ground brings out the elegance of the architecture even more… And then there are the glorious winter sunsets when the whole sky is coloured in disturbing shades of crimson and violet. It must be admitted, though, that there are not that many fine days in winter and everybody looks forward to spring with growing impatience. The arrival of the first sunny, spring-like days is like a fairy-tale awakening. Winter still reigns, there is still snow everywhere, but the sun is exceptionally brighter and it shines a little longer each day. The bright light pouring onto everything around heralds the inevitable approach of spring. The writer Mikhail Prishvin – a keen student of nature –

called this time in St Petersburg the "spring of light" and wrote of it: "It is astonishing how much poets' pens have laboured to depict St Petersburg's rains and fogs, damp, sticky snow and the unease of the White Nights. But why, as far as I can recall, have few turned their attention to the spring of light in this northern city, when the first heavenly light transforms the wonderful buildings still whitened with the snow of winter."

And spring itself is beautiful and poetic: the ice-floes on the Neva, the abundant greenery, the re-emergence of the flowers and fountains by the Kazan Cathedral, the glorious display of lilacs on the Field of Mars – it all puts Petersburgers and visitors to the city in a romantic mood.

The city, however, is best known, of course, for its White Nights, when its charm reveals itself with especial force and originality. In this period when dusk merges into dawn, St Petersburg acquires a slightly phantasmagoric look and it sometimes seems that the White Nights and the arched entrances to well-like St Petersburg courtyards were the inspiration for the metaphysical paintings of De Chirico with their unearthly, disturbing illumination and figures frozen as if in a dream.

The White Nights are noted for the traditional bridge-raising ritual so beloved of locals and visitors alike. It is one of the chief attractions of the summer tourist season, alongside the fountains of Peterhof and the masterpieces of the Hermitage. There is, it must be admitted, nothing particularly unusual in the

The Palace Bridge. 1912–16. Engineer Andrzej Pszenicki, architect Roman Meltser

The Bank Bridge across the Griboyedov Canal. 1825–26.
Engineer Georges Traitteur, sculptor Pavel Sokolov

spectacle itself: the bridges lift to allow large vessels that cannot otherwise get under them to pass to and from the Gulf of Finland. The procedure does not take long, but people gather on the embankments ahead of time to be sure of a good view. The slow rise of the central spans of the bridges stirs up general enthusiasm. The silhouettes of ships and barges dotted with lights appear through the gloom and grow gradually clearer as they approach. There is something inexplicably moving about the sight. The writer Vasily Rozanov, who lived in an apartment with a view of the Neva, recorded that late into the night his children loved to sit by the windows watching the lights of vessels passing by.

It is a well known fact that Peter forbade the construction of buildings taller than his own palace, the only exception being churches. Later buildings stayed much the same height out of a sense of proportion and good taste. As a consequence, the upper floors of the few taller buildings in the centre of St Petersburg enjoy a fine "bird's-eye view" across the roughly level rooftops of the city. Let us take a look at St Petersburg from, say, the window of some artist's studio – as a rule they

are located on the top floor or under a mansard roof. Old houses with irregular rows of chimneys long-since unused, unexpected combinations of colour in the metal sheeting and *brandmauer* dividing or blank walls, the unusual shapes of mansard roofs, the fascinating structure of the masonry in places where it has been laid bare, some new-fangled "flying-saucer" antennae, advertisements, parapets and sculptured decoration – the whole urban landscape evokes a highly picturesque feeling of Cubist multidimensionality, compressed space, the combination of the incompatible. And the domes, crosses and spires of familiar, instantly recognizable landmarks rising above the roofs endow the rather gloomy panorama with the vividness of some original slant on reality. Regrettably, there has recently been a trend to cover roofs with galvanized sheeting which introduces a discordant note into the motley appearance of the old city seen from above.

There is one more distinctive feature of St Petersburg – the old industrial outskirts, of which Alexander Blok was so fond and which figures largely in his poetry. On the Vyborg Side, on the Priazhka, where the poet's museum is now, and on the Obvodny Ca-

nal you can still find places where tall chimneys, large red-brick factory blocks and yellow barrack-like housing for the workers in the immediate proximity of a lesser canal or river create a rather gloomy atmosphere that is distinctively St Petersburg.

In general, there are a great many splendid corners hidden around the city, revealing themselves only to the curious pedestrian. One of them, known as "New Holland", is close to the place where Blok lived his last years. A long featureless building rises on a small island above the dark waters of the River Moika. Used at one time as timber warehouses, it is pierced by a huge, strikingly impressive arch. Even its present state of neglect does not detract from the poetic charm of this architectural daydream by Vallin de la Mothe.

St Petersburg, still remaining a city of trams, might indeed lay claim to the title "tram capital of the world". The majority of big cities have very few trams, or have done away with them altogether as an out-dated mode of transport that hinders a greater volume of traffic. From the technical point of view they probably are an anachronism, but the bright, mainly traditional red wagons rumbling through the streets add to the feeling of the city's uniqueness. In the cold half-light of a winter's morning you would stand at a stop waiting for a tram. The streets in St Petersburg are generally long and straight, so you can see quite a way. In better days the trams came one after another and each had its own combination of coloured lights at the front: two reds; blue and red; yellow and green… Each route had its own distinctive pattern following a tradition which is now sadly forgotten and you could rec-

ognize "your" tram long before it arrived. There was something typically St Petersburg about that: a little bit of a game, but also a certain warmth and concern for people's convenience.

Besides, for many Petersburgers the tram is a favourite means of transport, not only by force of habit, but also because of the opportunity it affords to observe the architecture, scenes of life and glimpses of nature drifting unhurriedly by the large windows. For those who constantly use public transport, the tram is also a place to meet people. The Western taste for individual isolation is not at all typical for Petersburgers: Russian tradition encourages them to enter into conversation. The locals are naturally very fond of their city and enjoy helping strangers to find their way around.

But the tram is nonetheless gradually passing from our lives. Many today prefer the faster Metro, and as the century draws to a close the motor-car is increasingly displacing the tram on our streets. It is an inevitable process: the horse-drawn tram has long faded into history, followed by coaches, carriages and carts.

When speaking of the sights of St Petersburg, mention must of course be made of its remarkable suburbs – the magnificent "necklace" of Imperial residences constructed around the northern capital. The opulent decoration of the palaces and expansive parks at Tsarskoye Selo, the "town of the Muses", whose glory was extolled by Pushkin's poetic genius; the fairy-tale spectacle of Peterhof with its unique fountains; the austere luxury of the palaces and beautiful views in the parks at Pavlovsk, Gatchina and Oranienbaum are all inseparably linked with the history of the city itself.

◀ *The "New Holland". 1765–80. Architects Savva Chevakinsky and Jean-Baptiste Vallin de la Mothe*

Portrait of Peter the Great. 1713 or 1716.
Painting by Benoît Coffre

The epic tale of the creation of St Petersburg is something unparalleled in the history not only of Russia, but of the world as a whole. When, after taking the Swedish fortress of Nyenskans on the Neva in 1703, Peter finally decided to construct a new capital city in the delta so as to do away at one fell swoop with the conservative attitudes of old Moscow, he founded a fortress on Zayachy Island. The date when the fortress was begun – 16 May 1703 – is taken to be the day of the city's foundation. St Petersburg was constructed with such a burst of enthusiasm, with such an unprecedented concentration of effort, that it is difficult to find any analogies, at least in Russian history. Something of the same scale of thinking could possibly be found in Lenin's plans for the radical transformation of Russia, which also had their beginnings in the city on the Neva, "the cradle of the revolution". It was not without cause that the poet Maximilian Voloshin wrote "The great Peter was the first Bolshevik", referring to the Tsar's determination to hurl Russia from the past into the future, to break with established traditions. While the Bolshevik grand plan is, however, today regarded as a failed utopia, Peter's tremendous undertaking was seen through to a brilliant conclusion. The scope of the work was truly gigantic. Peter issued a ban on masonry construction across the whole of Russia. Anyone travelling to St Petersburg was obliged to bring with them a fixed quantity of stones, or to pay a tax. The immense construction site grew not by the day, but by the hour. And soon the first outlines of the future city became visible. Construction began on Vasilyevsky Island. Le Blond planned the city as a sea-port, something along the lines of Peter's beloved Amsterdam, or perhaps Venice – canals were dug out along the streets and vessels were supposed to anchor in them to unload. Very soon, however, it became clear that in the harsh northern climate the Venetian way of doing things was unsuitable (despite that, St Petersburg is quite often referred to as "the Venice of the North"). Notwithstanding, Vasilyevsky Island, together with the Petrograd Side, was the core from which the city developed. Menshikov's palace (built for the governor of the new city, Peter's closest associate whom he had elevated from a commoner), the building of the Twelve Collegia (now the University) and the Kunstkammer are impressive works of architecture begun in the first years of St Petersburg's history, which still draw tourists today. Visitors and Petersburgers alike have a special affection for an unimposing brick building hidden by trees near the Peter and Paul Fortress. Within it stands the Log Cabin of Peter the Great, his first dwelling in the city, built for him in three days and carefully preserved for posterity. It is striking above all for its modesty, providing first-hand evidence of how undemanding the city's founder was in his domestic life. Admittedly another residence of more impressive size – the two-storey Summer Palace – was begun almost immediately on the opposite side of the Neva. It is believed that Peter started it in order to encourage others to build on that bank. This palace too is, incidentally, quite modest. Today it is one of the sights of the city, like everything else associated with its founder. Probably of even more interest are the Summer Gardens in which the palace stands. This fairly small patch of green, notable for its fine proportions, was planned out by the Tsar himself. It was a particularly happy idea of Peter's to decorate the gardens with Classical statues, the exquisite shapes and whiteness of which now contrasts splendidly with

The Menshikov Palace. 1710–27.
Architects Giovanni Fontana and Gottfried Schädel

The Twelve Collegia building (now St Petersburg University). 1722–42.
Architects Domenico Trezzini, Mikhail Zemtsov and Theodor Schwertfeger

◀ *The gate of the Summer Gardens. 1773–84.*
Architects Yury Velten and Piotr Yegorov

The Summer Palace of Peter the Great. 1710–14. Architect Domenico Trezzini

The Summer Gardens

Portrait of Empress Catherine I.
Between 1770 and 1800. Painting by Heinrich Buchholz

the old lime-trees and the austere pattern of the cast-iron railing created later by Velten. The charming Summer Gardens are one of the favourite places for Petersburgers to stroll, something already mentioned by Pushkin.

Yet, for all Peter's astonishing successes in constructing the city, far from everything went as smoothly as it might seem today. Tremendous achievements were the result of immense labour and numerous sacrifices. Tens of thousands of people were brought to the enormous construction site and many of them are believed to have succumbed to the back-breaking toil and pernicious climate. There has long been a saying that the city stands on bones. Peter operated by example, by his wits, but also by dint of persistence and force.

The chronicle of the St Petersburg period in Russia, from Peter's time on, is far from idyllic. It is full of striking contrasts and pages of tragedy. The Tsar who surrounded himself with foreigners, pitilessly rejected age-old national traditions, and forced a move to the marshy fringe of the state not only on common workers, but also on the nobility, high officials and craftsman earned himself the hatred of many. The Old Believers, who were especially severely persecuted by the Reformer-Tsar, saw him as the embodiment of the Antichrist. Peter's own son, Alexis, came out in opposition to his father's undertakings, but the reforms Russia vitally needed and St Petersburg as the living

The Palace Embankment. The railing of the Summer Gardens.
1773–84. Architects Yury Velten and Piotr Yegorov

Portrait of Emperor Peter II. 1728.
Painting by Johann Paul Lüdden

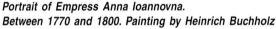

Portrait of Empress Anna Ioannovna.
Between 1770 and 1800. Painting by Heinrich Buchholz

Monument to Peter the Great (the "Bronze Horseman").
1766–82. Sculptor Etienne-Maurice Falconet

symbol of them were more important to Peter than anything and in order to preserve his life's cause he had to sacrifice even his son. The tragic scene of the furious Peter interrogating his recalcitrant son in the Palace of Monplaisir at Peterhof was vividly depicted by the nineteenth-century artist Nikolai Gay.

The moral climate in young St Petersburg was far from ideal. The activities of the notorious "All-joking, All-drinking Council of Fools and Jesters" parodying ecclesiastic tradition were little short of plain blasphemy. A certain justification for such amusements might possibly be that Peter and his associates, worn down by the pressure of continuous work, needed a diversion and such debauches brought relief from the excessively intensive efforts they put into construction. In play, as in work, Peter's time was marked by a truly titanic appetite, lack of restraint and lack of moderation. Peter's second wife was Martha Skavronskaya, a Livonian washerwoman picked up on one of the campaigns. Far from noble by pedigree and not of the highest morality, she was nonetheless destined soon to ascend the Russian throne under the name Catherine I.

Everything about Peter's reign is a mass of glaring contradictions. But posterity rapidly forgets shortcomings when it is surrounded by the tangible results of creative labour, and Peter I, who laid the foundations of not only St Petersburg but a whole new Russia became established in

Portrait of Empress Yelizabeth Petrovna. 1760.
Painting be Carle Vanloo

the popular memory as Peter the Great, creator of the Russian Empire, a ruler who vigorously and decisively directed the country into course of dynamic development on the heels of the greatest European powers. That is how he is depicted in the monument that stands by the Neva opposite Vasilyevsky Island. The "Bronze Horseman", brilliantly sculpted by the Frenchman Falconet, became one of the chief symbols of the city. But in a wider sense everything in St Petersburg leads us back to thoughts of its great founder.

Peter's early and unexpected death inevitably slowed the incredible pace of work that had built up. His failure to appoint an heir in keeping with his own new law on the succession was the source of much discord. The reign of Catherine I, elevated by the intrigues of influential courtiers, above all Menshikov, and especially the coronation of Peter's niece Anna Ioannovna, which was followed by the arrival in St Petersburg of a host of Livonian Germans on the make, are a cause for gloomy reflection. Perhaps the only tangible reminder of the inglorious rule of Anna and her all-powerful favourite Biron is a monument put up later by the Cathedral of St Sampsonius, where Prince Volynsky and his associates Khrushchev and Yeropkin (one of the first architects of the city) were buried after their execution for taking a stand against excessive German influence. Admittedly, it was after Anna Ioannovna's

The Kriukov Canal. View of the Cathedral of St Nicholas
and the Epiphany. 1753–62. Architect Savva Chevakinsky

View of the Winter Palace

Portrait of Emperor Peter III. Between 1770 and 1800. Painting by an unknown Russian painter

coming to the throne that the capital of Russia, transferred to Moscow by the short-lived Tsar Peter II in 1728, was returned to St Petersburg.

Things got better, though, in the reign of Peter's daughter Elizabeth, who came to power with the help of the Preobrazhensky Guards Regiment still loyal to her father's traditions. Despite her extreme frivolity and obsession with balls and costumes, she successfully advanced her father's cause. Under her Francesco Bartolomeo Rastrelli began building the present-day Winter Palace and the Smolny Cathedral, Chevakinsky constructed the Cathedral of St Nicholas, and Rastrelli completed a remarkable palace for the Empress at Tsarskoye Selo. Her reign also saw the opening of the Corps of Pages (providing education and training for sons of the nobility) and the Academy of Arts.

St Petersburg developed particularly rapidly under Catherine II. Although she was not of Russian origin and seized the throne illegally, was constantly embroiled in affairs of the heart and generously rewarded her favourites, was vain and at times inconsistent, Catherine proved a blessing for Russia as a whole, and for St Petersburg in particular. Considering herself the heir to Peter's ideas (she set up the famous equestrian statue to the city's founder) and seeking the laurels of an enlightened monarch, Catherine did much to consolidate

The Academy of Arts. 1764–72. Architects
Jean-Baptiste Vallin de la Mothe and Alexander Kokorinov

The Sheremetev Palace (the "Fontanka Palace"). 1750–55.
Architects Savva Chevakinsky and Fiodor Argunov

The Smolny Cathedral. 1748–64. ▶
Architect Francesco Bartolomeo Rastrelli

Portrait of Empress Catherine the Great. 1780s.
Painting by an unknown artist

Russia's might and to develop its capital. Under her, the city already acquired its basic shape and became increasingly an object of admiration for its Classical beauty.

Apart from everything else, Catherine put the collecting of works of art, that had begun in Peter's time, on a systematic basis. Sparing neither time nor expense, she laid the foundations for the now world-famous Hermitage museum. By the end of her reign there were more than 2,000 paintings in the Hermitage, including celebrated works by Titian, Rembrandt, Raphael and Poussin. At the same time large collections in other branches of art were also created.

A worthy monument to Catherine's brilliant reign was the monument set up in the centre of Nevsky Prospekt where she is presented encircled by those who furthered the glory of her age – Potemkin, Suvorov, Rumiantsev, Orlov, Bezborodko, Princess Dashkova, Derzhavin...

An unenviable lot befell Catherine's son, Emperor Paul I, who knew from an early age that his mother had had no small part in the murder of his father, the rightful tsar. Paul hated everything connected with Catherine and spent his adult years before he came to the throne at Gatchina, remote from St Petersburg. The brief reign of the irritable, intemperate Paul, marked by the imposition of barrack-like discipline and greater censorship, an obsession with drill and the introduction of German-style uniforms in the army, has usually been seen in a highly negative light by historians. Modern,

The Winter Palace.
The Jordan (Main) Staircase.
Architect Francesco
Bartolomeo Rastrelli. 1762.
Architect Vasily Stasov. 1831

The New Hermitage. ▶
Portico with atlantes. 1844–49.
Architect Leo von Klenze,
sculptor Alexander Terebenev

◄ The Winter Palace.
The Hall of Peter the Great
(the Small Throne Room).
1833. Architect Auguste
de Montferrand

The Winter Palace. The Malachite Room. 1839.
Architect Auguste de Montferrand

The New Hermitage. The Room of Italian Painting (the Large Skylight Room)

The Hermitage Museum.
The Litta Madonna. Ca. 1490–91.
Painting by Leonardo da Vinci

The Hermitage Museum.
The Room
of Leonardo da Vinci.
Architect Giacomo
Quarenghi. 1805–07.
Architect Andrei
Stakenschneider. 1858

The Winter Canal

Palace Square

Portrait of Emperor Paul I.
Between 1770 and 1800.
Painting by an unknown Russian artist

more objective research, however, paints a picture of a tragic figure rather than the deranged despot of earlier historiography. Hardly a single one of the rational reforms devised by Paul went beyond the planning stage.

The most tragic events are connected with the Mikhailovsky Castle which Paul had built for himself in St Petersburg, at the junction of the Rivers Moika and Fontanka. An equestrian statue of Peter the Great by Carlo Rastrelli (the architect's father) was set up in front of the castle. This work had been disparaged by Catherine II and that prompted Paul to give it a place of particular honour. The construction of castles was no part of the Russian architectural tradition. The rather gloomy building separated from its surroundings by rivers and moats, looked even stranger in St Petersburg. The suspicious Emperor intended it as a sort of impregnable fortress, capable of warding off the assassination of which he, not unjustly, lived in constant fear. Ironically, it was in the Mikhailovsky Castle, cut off from the rest of the city, that he died as the result of a court conspiracy with the tacit consent of his son.

The reign of Alexander I was marked by many fine achievements in architecture. The successful war against Napoleon, ending with victory for the allies and the triumphal entry of Russian troops into Paris led to a popular mood of elation and an increase in the Emperor's popularity. Major edifices constructed under

Monument to Peter the Great. 1743–47. Sculptor Carlo Bartolomeo Rastrelli ▶

The Mikhailovsky (Engineers') Palace. 1797–1800.
Architects Vasily Bazhenov and Vincenzo Brenna

George Dawe. Portrait of the Emperor Alexander I. 1825

Alexander were Thomas de Thomon's Exchange, Quarenghi's Smolny Institute for the Daughters of the Nobility, Rossi's Yelagin Palace and Zakharov's new Admiralty. In 1811 Voronikhin built the Kazan Cathedral, a major landmark in the very middle of Nevsky Prospekt. Alexander's reign also saw the opening of the Tsarskoye Selo Lyceum and the Mining Institute. His memory is perpetuated by a monumental column on Palace Square. Late in 1825 Alexander suddenly died in distant Taganrog. There is still a persistent legend that the mystically inclined Tsar did not die, but assumed the identity of the wandering holy-man Fiodor Kuzmich. The main reason for such a move was supposedly repentance for his part in his father's death.

The Emperor's unexpected death prompted the arm uprising of the "Decembrists", a conspiracy of officers who favoured a French-style republic. The revolt was rapidly put down. Nicholas I, who now came to power, was a man of strictly conservative outlook. His reign saw the introduction of the reactionary slogan "Orthodoxy, Autocracy, National Spirit". The ideas of absolute monarchy which Nicholas undeviatingly pursued provoked extreme dissatisfaction in society. He was criticized by both the "Westernizers", liberal supporters of European-style democratic development, and the "Slavophiles" who looked to national traditions. The critics were undoubtedly correct on one score: harsh conservatism and the imposition of bureaucratic practices gradually led to the alienation of the authorities from the people and fuelled a strong strain of nihilism which became an unstoppable movement in the years after Nicholas's death.

View of the Admiralty. Early 19th century.
Tinted lithograph by Ferdinand Perrot

The central tower of the Admiralty. 1806–23. ▶
Architect Andrian Zakharov

The Yelagin Palace. Architect Giacomo Quarenghi. 1780s.
Architect Carlo Rossi. 1818–22

◄ *Palace Square. The General Staff building.*
1819–29. Architect Carlo Rossi

The Alexander Column. 1830–34.
Architect Auguste de Montferrand, sculptor Boris Orlovsky

Portrait of Emperor Nicholas I.
1849. Painting by Yegor Botman

It is a striking fact, however, that Nicholas's reign saw the flowering of Pushkin's genius and the emergence of such talents as Zhukovsky, Gogol, Griboyedov, Turgenev and Dostoyevsky. And St Petersburg too has no cause to complain of him: the key ensembles created by Rossi (Palace Square, the Senate and Synod, the Alexandrinsky Theatre), Montferrand (St Isaac's Square) and Thomas de Thomon (the Spit of Vasilyevsky Island) which to a considerable extent determine the majestic appearance of the northern capital were formed under Nicholas. The Tsar's favourite architect was Konstantin Thon, whose many creations in St Petersburg and Moscow include the terminuses of the railway connecting the two capitals, two buildings in a single style.

The crowning glory of Nicholas's reign was the immense Cathedral of St Isaac of Dalmatia, one of the main architectural sights of St Petersburg. The building, towering above the whole city, can hold some 13,000 people and is remarkable for the richness of its interior decoration. The view of the city from the colonnade beneath the dome creates an unforgettable impression. Almost the same time as the cathedral was completed, the sculptor Piotr Klodt finished work on the equestrian monument to Nicholas I that was set up facing St Isaac's. Despite a certain cool pomposity, the monument to the reactionary autocrat displays a fine crispness of line and an abundance of decorative detail.

The Mariinsky Theatre. Architect Albert Cavos. 1847–59.
Architect Victor Schröter. 1880

The Bolshoi Theatre. Early 19th century.
Watercolour by an unknown artist

The Mariinsky Theatre. The Tsar's box

St Isaac's Cathedral. 1818–58.
Architect Auguste de Montferrand

Monument to Nicholas I. 1856–59.
Sculptors Piotr Klodt, Robert Salemann
and Nikolai Ramazanov,
architect Auguste de Montferrand

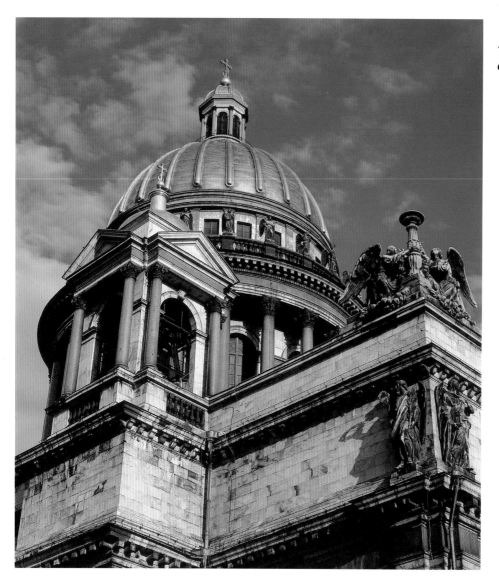

The dome
of St Isaac's

Detail of St Isaac's
interior

St Isaac's Square ▶

Portrait of Emperor Alexander II. 1876.
Painting by Nikolai Sverchkov

Alexander II, who succeeded Nicholas, has gone down in history as the "Liberator-Tsar". In 1861 he issued a decree finally abolishing serfdom. By a wicked irony of fate, however, the revolutionary movement which had by now become an end in itself selected this Tsar in particular as a target for assassination. It took many attempts before the terrorists eventually succeeded. In memory of Alexander II, the magnificent Church of the Resurrection of Christ, popularly known as "Our Saviour-on-the-Spilt-Blood", was constructed on the site of the fatal attack, close to Nevsky Prospekt. For all its exotic mix of architectural elements, some borrowed from St Basil's Cathedral in Moscow, this church attracts general attention with its expressive shape and the richness of its decoration, particularly the mosaics. Among the noted painters involved in their creation were Victor Vasnetsov and Mikhail Nesterov.

Railing of the Mikhailovsky Garden near the Church of the Resurrection of Christ. 1905–07. Architect Alfred Parland

The Church of the Resurrection ▶
of Christ ("Our Saviour-
on-the-Spilt-Blood"). 1883–1907.
Architects Archimandrite Ignaty
(Malyshev) and Alfred Parland

The cupolas of the Church of the Resurrection of Christ

Portrait of Emperor Alexander III. 1889.
Painting by Piotr Zabolotsky

Alexander III, who followed his father on the throne, pursued a more conservative course. Under him the country developed rapidly along capitalist lines, a process symbolized by the building of the immense Transsiberian Railway. Intensive construction took place in St Petersburg too. Many luxurious palaces, rich mansions and places of worship were built in this period, but they were not notable for particular originality or for unity of style. The dominant styles were eclecticism, historicism and the "Pseudo-Russian" manner. Alexander III's initiative led to the opening of the Russian Museum which became the greatest repository of the nation's own art, with famous paintings by Ivanov, Venetsianov, Shishkin, Aivazovsky, Repin, Surikov, Vrubel and many others.

Our image of Alexander III today is to a large extent shaped by the unusual equestrian monument to him created by the original sculptor Paolo Troubetskoi at the beginning of this century. This monument – squat, expressive and, evidently, truthful – was so strikingly dissimilar to the grand equestrian monuments to other monarchs that many perceived it as a caricature on the reactionary Tsar. It is among the many paradoxes of the Soviet era that this monument, which originally stood on the square in front of the Moscow Railway Station, was removed (it has recently found a new home in the courtyard of the Marble Palace, a branch of the Russian Museum), while the monument to Nicholas I, for example, despite its vainglorious display of a far more monarchist spirit, was left untouched.

The Russian Museum.
1819–25. Architect
Carlo Rossi

Monument to
Alexander Pushkin. 1957.
Sculptor Mikhail Anikushin,
architect Vasily Petrov

The Marble Palace. ▶
1768–85. Architect
Antonio Rinaldi

Monument
to Alexander III.
1906–09. Sculptor
Paolo Troubetskoy

The Russian Museum.
The Last Day of Pompeii. 1833.
Painting by Karl Briullov

The Russian Museum.
Portrait of the Poet
Anna Akhmatova. 1914.
Painting by Nathan Altman

The Russian Museum. The White Hall ▶
Architect Carlo Rossi

54

Portrait of the Emperor Nicholas II.
1900s–1910s.
Painting by Ernst Liphart

The destiny of the last Tsar in the Romanov dynasty, Nicholas II, who ascended the throne in 1892, proved to be the most tragic. There are no monuments to him in the city (a bust recently unveiled at Tsarskoye Selo is the only exclusion) and his reign has for the most part left only sad memories. The bad omens began immediately after the coronation in Moscow, when a crush among the ordinary people who had gathered on Khodynka Field to greet the new Tsar resulted in many fatalities. Then came the defeat in the Russo-Japanese War and January 1905 when troops opened fire on peaceful demonstrators, triggering the first, abortive revolution... In 1911 came the fateful assassination of the energetic prime-minister Stolypin who had embarked on some highly promising reforms, on completion of which he envisaged a truly "great Russia". Then followed the First World War, the decline in the Imperial family's authority due to association with Rasputin, abdication and, finally, the October Revolution and the dreadful death of the entire family...

Aesthetically, Nicholas's reign saw the emergence of the Art Nouveau, known in Russia as *moderne*, in St Petersburg's architecture. The Trinity Bridge was constructed and a building boom gripped the Petrograd Side, which had long been considered one of the quiet outskirts. Many of the buildings on the Petrograd Side display a more modern style. A vivid example is the

The arch of Mathilda Kschessinska's
mansion. 1904–06. Architect
Alexander von Gogen

mansion constructed for the ballerina Mathilda Kschessinska not far from the Peter and Paul Fortress. This creation of Alexander von Hogen is marked by whimsical ornament and emphatic asymmetry.

The Bolshevik seizure of power was the beginning of a totally unique period in the life of the entire country, including St Petersburg. The striving to decisively make over the past, and do away above all with the traces of monarchy and religion, led to great losses in the arts. Moscow suffered most, having become the capital of the country again in 1918. St Petersburg, by then already Petrograd and soon, after Lenin's death in 1924, to become Leningrad, was somewhat more fortunate, but here too a large number of places of worship and historical monuments were demolished. Most badly affected, though, was the cultural life of the northern capital. The majority of aristocratic families, the most educated section of society, and many artists, writers and musicians fled abroad. In 1922 even those major thinkers and opinion-makers who had remained were expelled from the country.

But the coming of the new social order was also accompanied by great achievements in the arts. It was the enthusiasm of the first post-revolutionary years that gave a powerful impetus to the development of experimental trends in Russian art, a phenomenon which achieved international recognition. The world's first institute for the study of modern art was created in St Petersburg. Malevich, Kandinsky, Tatlin and oth-

er famous innovative artists worked there. The avant-garde movement was admittedly soon reduced to nothing by the pressure of censorship, but it survived long enough to another remarkable phenomenon: the Leningrad school of children's book design. The Leningrad publishing house headed by the artist Vladimir Lebedev managed to utilize the achievements of "left-wing" experimental art in the realm of book illustration, creating children's books of the highest aesthetic standard. The publications designed by Lebedev himself, Vera Yermolayeva, Alexei Pakhomov, Nikolai Tyrsa and other Leningrad-based artists were a milestone in the art of the book worldwide.

Despite the radical change in the country's way of life, losses and repressions, in the 1930s a new atmosphere gradually formed: a joyful spirit of creation coupled with confidence in a brighter future. Leningraders, as the city's inhabitants now proudly styled themselves, were still notable for their cultured manners. This was no mere coincidence: the former capital still possessed a large number of educated, well brought-up people. A special atmosphere of kindness and intelligence reigned and a sort of unwritten Leningrad code of conduct established itself, governing the way people lived and interacted. Leningraders loved their city and took a pride in it.

These special qualities came to the fore in the war years, when Leningrad found itself encircled by enemy forces. The siege is an indelible page in the history of the city, evoking particular respect for the courage

◀ *A building in the Art Nouveau style on the Petrograd Side*

Mathilda Kschessinska's mansion. 1904–06.
Architect Alexander von Gogen

Fetching Water on the Neva. 1942. Lithograph by Alexei Pakhomov. From the series "During the Siege"

was fortunate: in contrast to Moscow new construction was carried out mainly in previously empty districts and the glorious historical centre of the city was left untouched. Even the occasional intrusions there were not particularly disastrous, as the strong sense of harmonious unity prevented the construction of anything strongly at odds with the legacy of past ages. One of the greatest successes was Mikhail Anikushin's monument to Pushkin, which made the square in front of the Russian Museum splendidly complete.

In the late 1980s Russia entered another "revolutionary" phase. In 1991, following a referendum, St Petersburg again acquired its historical name. For those who grew up under Soviet rule, "Petersburg" did not roll easily off the tongue, sounding too self-important, old-fashioned and somehow "un-Russian". Moreover, in contrast to the old practice, it became common in all situations, formal or informal, to speak of "Saint Petersburg", which sounded even more pretentious. The debate over the renaming was heated: not only die-hard Communists, but many inhabitants remote from politics could not reconcile themselves to the old-new name. Although passions still run high on the question, the matter is now settled and it only remains for the population to live up to the name. As yet, sadly, the longer we live in "St Petersburg", the more we are aware of the glaring contrast between the lofty name of the city and its present condition. Now, when Petersburg-Petrograd-Leningrad, having gone through revolutions and siege, is again being sorely tried, let us trust that the proud name of "St Petersburg" will become celebrated not only because of the great history of the city, but also on account of new accomplishments to which the unfading beauty of old St Petersburg must inevitably inspire us.

of its citizens in this country and abroad. There are still living witnesses to the events that led to the tragic death of almost a million Leningraders. For well over two years, the city resisted the onslaught of Nazi forces. Hundreds of thousands died of starvation, but the heroic city never did surrender. This act of unparalleled heroism is commemorated by a host of memorials, the main one of which is the Piskariovskoye Cemetery complex, where many of those who died in the siege lie buried in mass graves. Respect for the memory of loved ones is a characteristic feature of Petersburgers. Following long established tradition as the Victory Day (9 May) holiday draws close, on "Parents' Saturday" especially, they visit the city's cemeteries to place flowers on the graves.

A disproportionate number of siege victims were representatives of the old St Petersburg intelligentsia, already getting on in years and never particularly practically minded. The brutally depopulated city was resettled by outsiders and celebrated St Petersburg traditions were to a large extent lost. Yet as the damaged buildings were restored, the city again began to look like the Russian northern capital. Especially extensive work was required on the suburban residences which had been behind the German lines and destroyed almost entirely during the retreat. Today they are all resplendent in their former glory and it is hard for the delighted tourists to imagine the true extent of the devastation and the efforts it cost to restore these magnificent ensembles.

In the course of post-war development, attention was concentrated on the purely utilitarian task of providing the population with housing and that, in conjunction with strict ideological restrictions, regrettably conspired against the construction of monuments and great works of architecture worthy to stand alongside the superb survivals of the past. Yet here again the city

To a Hospital. 1942. Lithograph by Alexei Pakhomov. From the series "During the Siege"

The memorial at the Piskariovskoye Cemetery ▶

In order to really understand St Petersburg, to grasp its spirit, you have to view it as a single whole, to examine the main architectural complexes which formed over time and determined the face of Russia's northern capital. An excursion around any city begins as a rule with the central square. In St Petersburg that is Palace Square. The best point from which to view the square is the corner farthest away from Nevsky Prospekt, where Millionnaya Street begins. From there you have a splendid panorama. In the centre is the remarkable Alexander Column which, as any guide will tell you, is held up only by its own weight. The astonishingly expressive figure of an angel with a cross on the top of the column is the work of the sculptor Boris Orlovsky. But the immense square itself creates a harmonious impression, despite the contrasting elements which frame it: the militarily uniform white-and-yellow official buildings created by Rossi and Rastrelli's avowedly artistic and irregular Winter Palace with sculpture on the parapet, the gilded dome of the palace church, white half-columns and black-grilled gates against the pale green background of the walls. A special role in the ensemble is played by the celebrated arch of the General Staff building, which interacts positively with the regular rhythm of the building and, of course, by the chariot of glory above it which endows the whole monumental structure with a sense of artistic perfection and even airiness.

Away to the left of Palace Square is the start of the city's main thoroughfare, Nevsky Prospekt. In order to get a feel of the city, you should walk it from one end to the other because this is the quintessence of St Petersburg, the symbol of its outstanding historical culture. It is not only that "Nevsky" is the city's central street, on and around which are located many theatres, museums, publishing houses, hotels and im-

◀ **Angel crowning the Alexander Column.**
1831–32. Sculptor Boris Orlovsky

View of the Alexander Column
through the Arch of the General Staff building

The Griboyedov Canal

The Wolf and Beranger Grocery. Early 19th century. Tinted lithograph by an unknown artist

The Cathedral of Our Lady of Kazan. 1801–11.
Architect Andrei Voronikhin

The Yeliseyev Shop. 1901–03.
Architect Gavriil Baranovsky

The Alexandrine Theatre. 1828–32.
Architect Carlo Rossi,
sculptors Vasily Demuth-Malinovsky,
Stepan Pimenov and Alessandro Triscorni

Monument to Catherine the Great. 1862–73.
Sculptors Matvei Chizhov and
Alexander Opekushin, architects
Mikhail Mikeshin and David Grimm

The Chernyshev (Lomonosov)
Bridge. 1785–87

portant shops, the National Library of Russia and even the most important railway terminus (on the line to Moscow); not even that it is adorned by such remarkable works of architecture as the Kazan Cathedral, the Anichkov and Stroganov Palaces and the Alexandrinsky Theatre – every building here is part of the history of the city. In one way or another the lives of almost all poets, writers, artists and performers are connected with Nevsky. Those who really know the city can talk for hours about this one street. Take, for example, Beranger's pastry-shop, where Pushkin called in on the way from his home on the nearby Moika to the place of the fateful duel. Or the former Wawelberg bank building, modelled on the Palace of the Doges – when it was first put up in 1912 people complained that its massive forms overpowered its more modest neighbours, and the Venetian motifs were too pretentious. Time, however, has shown otherwise and today no-one would deny that it is one of the gems of Nevsky Prospekt. Or the palace designed in the florid Baroque style by the fa-

mous Rastrelli for the Stroganov family, which housed their remarkable collection of icons, paintings and applied art…

Near its middle, Nevsky broadens out into a small square around the monument to Catherine the Great. On one side the square is flanked by the Anichkov Palace, built for Empress Elizabeth's favourite Alexei Razumovsky, afterwards given to Potemkin, later the preferred residence of Alexander III. On the other is the city's exceptionally conveniently located main library, popularly known simply as the "Publichka", through whose doors nearly all the city's notable inhabitants must at one time have passed. At the back of the square stands its chief adornment, the Classically shaped Alexandrinsky Theatre, created by the brilliant Rossi. A proper impression of the talent of that outstanding master can be obtained from the street running from behind the theatre which now bears his name. Its width is precisely the same as the height of the buildings, twenty-two metres, and its length is exactly

View of the University Embankment and the Spit of Vasilyevsky Island

ten times that figure. This superb application of Classical proportions cannot fail to leave anyone unmoved.

The exotic building across Nevsky from the square was built with a sense of style typical of the merchant class by the Yeliseyevs. The luxurious Art Nouveau interior of their shop completely fulfils the promise held out by the façade punctuated by a huge window and allegorical figures of Trade and Industry.

Nevsky was and remains the focal point of city life. From morning until late evening its broad pavements are full of people. Anyone living in St Petersburg finds himself caught up from time to time in this endless flow of pedestrians, some hurrying about their business, others simply enjoying a stroll. Quite often you bump into an acquaintance while walking in this crowd. Nevsky Prospekt is associated with the dynamism of life in St Petersburg both in the time of Gogol, who described the capital's main street in a celebrated story, and in the present day.

One of the most remarkable places in the city is the Spit of Vasilyevsky Island. It is interesting in itself, but

also for the superb panoramic view it affords and for the host of museums and architectural monuments in the vicinity. One's attention is drawn here above all to the Rostral Columns. They were put up in 1810 to the design of Thomas de Thomon. In emulation of a Roman tradition the ships' prows (*rostra*) symbolize Russian naval victories. The gentle ramps descending to the water of the Neva which flank the columns on either side are superbly conceived and decoratively finished. The Rostral Columns form part of an ensemble, the key element of which is the Exchange building (now the Naval Museum), which Thomas de Thomon modelled on a Grecian temple. The neighbouring buildings, once warehouses, now house the Zoological Museum and the Museum of Soil Science. A little way along the embankment is the Institute of Russian Literature (the "Pushkin House") which contains priceless manuscripts by the country's outstanding writers.

It might be said that this area is in a way the intellectual centre of the city. A walk from the Spit along

The Chesme Church. 1777–80
Architect Yury Velten

The Spit of Vasilyevsky Island
The Rostral Column

The St Alexander Nevsky Lavra.
The Cathedral of the Holy Trinity.
1776–90. Architect Ivan Starov

The Peter and Paul Fortress

Portrait of Alexander Pushkin. 1827.
Painting by Vasily Tropinin

University Embankment which follows the main course of the Neva is sufficient proof of this. Immediately after the corner is the Kunstkammer, a building originally intended to house Peter's collection of curiosities. Today it is the Museum of Ethnography of the Peoples of the World. The building also contains the Museum of Lomonosov, the "spiritual son" of Peter the Great, whose reforms enabled this peasant's son to become a great scientist. Farther on stands the Classical building of the Academy of Sciences. Placed end on to the embankment is the unusually long two-storey building of the university, originally built by Trezzini for the Twelve Collegia, or ministries, of Peter's day. It is notable too for the single corridor that runs more than a half of the 400-metre length of the second storey – almost too far for the eye to see!

Farther along the embankment is the splendid palace constructed for Peter's boon companion Alexander Menshikov, today another museum. Then comes the Academy of Arts, *alma mater* to practically all Russia's greatest artists. Close to the Academy, on the granite-clad bank of the Neva, two majestic sphinxes brought from Egypt in the nineteenth century have found a happy second home. It should be noted that all along the embankment there is a striking view of the opposite

The Memorial Museum
"Alexander Pushkin's Last Flat". The Study

side of the river with the Admiralty, the Bronze Horseman, St Isaac's and another of Rossi's memorable ensembles – the Senate and Synod buildings.

Mention must certainly be made of one of the city's most important historical and architectural monuments – the Peter and Paul Fortress, whose main entrance is from the direction of Trinity Square. The name of the square, and of the bridge that runs from it across the Neva, commemorates the Trinity Cathedral, Peter the Great's favourite place of worship, which once stood here. The wooden building has sadly not survived. It burned down in 1913 and was restored after the revolution only to be demolished. Running straight as an arrow from Trinity Square is Kamennoostrovsky Prospekt, flanked by many attractive buildings.

Peter himself played a significant part in the planning of the Peter and Paul Fortress, the historical core of the city. Its contours were determined by the shape of the island on which it stands. Bastions named after Peter and some of his closest companions were linked by thick curtain walls. The original earth-and-log structure had been wholly replaced by masonry by 1740. The work was directed by the city's first chief architect, Domenico Trezzini. Although built for military purposes, the fortress in fact never saw action, but for many years it served as a prison. Among the first inmates of this "Russian Bastille" was Peter's son Alexis. Later the Decembrists were held here and many other political prisoners languished in its walls. By an irony of fate, almost all the Russian rulers were buried in the fortress, inside the SS Peter and Paul Cathedral, almost within sight of the prison bastions. The main lane in the fortress leads to the cathedral and the Grand-Ducal Burial Chapel constructed alongside at the turn of the twentieth century. The cathedral was built between 1712 and 1733 in the early Baroque style to Trezzini's design and is more reminiscent of Western European Protestant churches than traditional Russian ones. The spire on its bell-tower soars to 122.5 metres, making it the tallest structure in the city, apart from the television tower. Close by the cathedral is the Boat-House constructed to keep the "grandfather of the Russian navy", the small vessel in which Peter the Great learnt to sail. Across the cobbled

square is the squat, two-storey building of the Mint where coins and medals have been produced since the eighteenth century. It still functions today. In 1991 an unusual monument to Peter I by the contemporary artist and sculptor Mikhail Shemiakin was set up in the fortress. It provoked great debate on whether these historical precincts were the right place to display an "avantgarde" work of art.

There is not enough space here to describe even briefly all the main sights of St Petersburg – they are so thick on the ground in the central part of the city and so

Alexander Benois. Frontispiece for the poem
"The Bronze Horseman" by Alexander Pushkin. 1905

Pier with sphinxes on the University Embankment near the Academy of Arts. 1832–34. Architect Konstantin Thon

Pier near the Academy of Arts. Early 19th century. Tinted lithograph by Ferdinand Perrot

*Lantern at
the Panteleimonovsky
Bridge. 1909–11.
Architect Lev Ilyin*

*Standard lamp
on the First Engineers'
Bridge. 1828–29.
Engineer Pierre Bazin*

The interior of the SS Peter and Paul Cathedral

*Monument to Peter the Great. 1991.
Sculptor Mikhail Shemiakin*

many historical events are associated with them. A short reference must, though, be made to Peterhof – Peter's primary summer residence which he himself helped to design. The Grand Palace, felicitously sited on a tall coastal ridge, enjoys a splendid view of the Gulf of Finland. From below it, a canal runs straight to the sea, flanked by some of Peterhof's 140 fountains sparkling in the sun. Ships pass by out in the Gulf, in a slow, dignified manner. Built into the steep slope beneath the palace is the Great Cascade, one of the largest arrangements of fountains in the world. Sixty-four separate jets spring upwards here. In the central basin stands the celebrated sculptural group of *Samson Tearing Open the Jaws of the Lion*. It symbolizes Russia's victory in the Northern War against Sweden. Below, the Lower Park extends for several miles along the seashore. It contains a number of lesser palaces and pavilions adorned by cascades, grottoes, flower-beds, sculptures and, of course, fountains, among which the trick-fountains are always especially popular with visitors. Above, behind the palace, there is one more large, and no less attractive park. The majesty and scale of Peterhof delight and fascinate people from all over the world.

The only possible rival to Peterhof among the suburban Imperial residences is Tsarskoye Selo. It is not so much the fact that there you can find magnificent palaces and enchanting parks with pavilions, pergolas, monuments, ponds and lakes. Tsarskoye Selo derives its special charm from its association with Pushkin. If one can speak of a "general idol" in Russia, then the prime candidate for the title must be Pushkin. It is hopeless to try to explain to someone who does not know Russian the virtues of his poetry, which does not lend itself to translation, still less the prominent position he occupies in the minds of his countrymen and -women. Pushkin who combined within him the culture of the West and a love of the unprepossessing Russian landscape, the refinement of a European and the directness of an ordinary Russian, the lofty ideals of Christianity and a Hellenic zest for a full life, is above all, to use Dostoyevsky's expression, the embodiment of our "universal responsiveness". Pushkin became the most complete representative of the Russian ideal, and St Petersburg where European civilization and Russian culture met is a truly Pushkinesque city. "To the challenge thrown down by Peter, Russia replied a hundred years later with the tremendous phenomenon that was Pushkin" – that is how the poet's significance for Russia is described. No-one sang the praises of the city on the Neva and its creator, con-

Sphinx on the Egyptian Bridge. 1825–26. Sculptor Pavel Sokolov

Pushkin. The Catherine Palace.
Architect Francesco Bartolomeo
Rastrelli. 1752–56

Peterhof. The Great Palace. 1755. ▶
Architect Francesco Bartolomeo Rastrelli

The Great Cascade.
Architects Jean-Baptiste Le Blond,
Johann Braunstein, Niccolo Michetti
and Francesco Bartolomeo Rastrelli

The Samson Fountain. 1802.
Architect Mikhail Kozlovsky

veyed so profoundly both the greatness of Peter's deeds and the tragic aspect of his epoch-making age, like Pushkin.

St Petersburg was witness to the last, most mature years of the poet's life; witness too, sadly, to the duel that cut short his life. The melancholy, then remote site of the encounter on the Black River is marked by an obelisk. Indeed all places associated with Pushkin in the city are carefully preserved. Of particular interest is his last apartment on the Moika. No less revered is the Tsarskoye Selo Lyceum where he got his education and the town that sprang up around the Imperial residence now bears the poet's name.

Of course, St Petersburg's attraction lies not only in its physical monuments, but also in its association with the finest achievements of Russian culture. Its streets call to mind some of the outstanding works by Russian authors. Nevsky Prospekt is more than pretty in itself, but it gains even more fascination from the role it plays in the classics of literature. It seems that at any moment a carriage will come bowling down Nevsky, with Gogol's mystical Nose (which ran away from its owner) riding proudly in the back, while the Bronze Horseman, that symbol of St Petersburg, appears forever on the point of chasing of down the embankment in pursuit of some "Poor Yevgeny" dissatisfied with the Tsar's creation, just like in Pushkin's poem.

And these literary associations amount to far more than just a poetic perception of the architecture or history of St Petersburg. They add depth to the image of the city, giving it extra dimensions and interest. St Petersburg is capable of evoking gloomy moods as well as delight. One often clearly pictures the bureaucratic machinery of state, the endless ministries and institutions of Nicholas I's capital with their complete disregard for the individual and recalls the literary representatives of the St Petersburg civil service, from Akaky Akakiyevich to Makar Devushkin, Dostoyevsky's archetypal "little man". Dostoyevsky in general is a writer with a very St Petersburg spirit. His characters involuntarily spring to mind, for example, on many of the little streets around Sennaya Square.

The site selected for St Petersburg, on the low-lying, marshy banks of a broad northern river, often threatened by floods, gives it a certain air of unreality. The unpredictable St Petersburg weather, with its biting winds and fogs that wrap everything around in a whitish haze, intensifies this sense of the city as something of unstable, fantastic, artificial origin. The incredibly short time span in which the capital was built, its dissimilarity to the rest of Russia and its position on the very edge of the state, as well as the emphatic regularity of its architecture also encouraged the formation of a distinctive St Petersburg mythology in literature. There was, for example, a legend, recorded by the writer Vladimir Odoyevsky, that Peter first built the city in its entirety to a single plan and only then lowered it to the earth, so that it did not sink into the marsh.

The massive Classical buildings of the administrative capital of the Empire used for activities bureaucratically remote from real life also put one in a particular mood. Dostoyevsky, who keenly sensed the spirit of the city, wrote vividly of the fantastic quality of "regular" St Petersburg. The same sense of unreality was developed further in the Symbolist myth of the city on the Neva. The literary works of Alexander Blok, Andrei Bely and Dmitry Merezhkovsky reflect not only the attractive features of Peter's creation, but also those mysterious, disturbing moods that the city's appearance can inspire.

St Petersburg was the centre of Russian Symbolism. At the turn of the century an exceptionally productive atmosphere existed here, in which artists, poets, thinkers and architects joined forces. It is with good cause that this period in Russian culture has become known as the "Silver Age". In the northern capital it was marked by intensive religious and philosophical searchings, and refinement in literature and the arts. Of immense importance in bringing together those active in different cultural fields was the *World of Art*, a journal that appeared at this time. It is, of course, no coincidence that the World of Art as a creative association with its emphasis on the aesthetic, its cult of refinement and tendency towards stylization appeared in St Petersburg rather than anywhere else, in the same way that the vivid, unrestrained Jack of Diamonds group was a natural product of Moscow. The emphatic geometricality of the city on the Neva, the precision and severity of its lines, and the fine gradations of its colouring inevitably gave rise to a whole host of graphic artists who perpetuated its beauty.

The *World of Art* not only brilliantly channelled the efforts of the finest artists, thinkers and writers, but also served as a first step in the organizational career of Sergei Diaghilev, who became known to the world through his triumphant series of the "Russian Seasons" in Paris and other European cities. Sets, music and superb dancing were presented to the audience as a gloriously harmonious whole. The solo performers of the Mariinsky Theatre – Pavlova, Nijinsky, Karsavina – became internationally famous. The ballet music of Mussorgsky, Rimsky-Korsakov, Tchaikovsky and Stravinsky won Western hearts not only because it was brilliantly performed, but also because it was enhanced by the fairy-tale sets and costumes designed by Bakst, Benois, Bilibin, Golovin and many other St Petersburg artists who worked for the theatre.

Today St Petersburg is in a period of transition. Some things are noticeably undergoing a revival; others are being neglected and abandoned. Yet there can be no doubting that a city with such a glorious historical and cultural past, a city of such unsurpassed beauty will breath new life into the best traditions of former days...

Valery Fateyev